Award-winning comedian Jeff Green is one of the most popular comics working in the UK today. He has staged several sell-out tours in the West End and throughout Britain and Australia. He appears regularly on television shows such as *Never Mind the Buzzcocks* and *Have I Got News For You*, and has starred in several TV specials of his own. He lives in London with his partner.

JEFF GREEN

The A–Z of
Living Together

A Survival Guide for Cohabiting Lovers
(Or Kinky Friends . . .!)

timewarner
paperbacks

A *Time Warner* Paperback

First published in Great Britain by
Time Warner Paperbacks in 2002
Reprinted 2002 (four times)

For further information about Jeff Green visit
www.jeffgreen.co.uk and
www.offthekerb.co.uk

A CIP catalogue record for this book is available
from the British Library.

ISBN 0 7515 3379 3

Typeset in Berkeley by M Rules
Printed and bound in Great Britain by
Clays Ltd, St Ives plc

Time Warner Paperbacks
An imprint of
Time Warner Books UK
Brettenham House
Lancaster Place
London WC2E 7EN

www.TimeWarnerBooks.co.uk

For Fiona and Glen

'For a Male and Female to live continuously together is . . . biologically speaking, an extremely unnatural condition'

ROBERT BRIFFAULT

'Men and women should live next door to each other and visit regularly'

KATHARINE HEPBURN

Foreword by Jo Brand

Welcome to Jeff Green's *A–Z of Living Together*.

You may be wondering what credentials Jeff possesses – what endows him with the authority to pen a book about the coupling of the fair sex with the hairy sex. (And I don't necessarily mean who you think I mean.) Let me tell you.

I have known Jeff for a very long time indeed. Much of that time has been spent travelling the length and breadth of this island in sweaty cars in order to entertain the masses with stand-up comedy. In fact, I feel I know Jeff *so* well that I could almost have lived with him, except that we haven't stabbed each other or attempted to drown each other's pets. Judging also by the cavalcade of distressed women Jeff has left in his wake, I feel he has at least had plenty of experience in this area, if not always of the right sort.

In the world of comedy books, men tend to portray women as desperate neurotics with wedding dresses on under their crop tops, and women tend to portray men as commitment-phobic ejaculation machines. In comparison, Jeff has managed to strike a nice balance between the sexes, and the very special role each has to play in the total nuclear destruction of the relationship. We are led through pages embracing such disparate topics as 'Lipstick', 'Chores' and 'Selective Blindness', each one revealing a well-honed insight into all our personal failings as naturally heat-seeking human beings.

Having experienced the 'living together' phenomenon myself on several occasions, I now realise that, had I been able to peruse Jeff's book earlier, I could have improved huge sections of my life. I suppose I will just have to learn to live with the tortured memories.

Jeff has put his finger on the painful, yet hysterically funny (as we all know tragedy is) pulse of a live-in relationship. Hopefully this, his first learned discourse, will prevent many of you from falling at the first hurdle. (Though if your partner is making you compete against them in the 110 metre high-hurdles, I would *seriously* think about chucking them in any case.)

Jo Brand

Introduction

Hello, and welcome to the wonderful world of Cohabitation!

Almost all of us will, at some point in our lives, choose to live romantically with someone else – if only to say 'I did it once, now leave me alone with my cats.'

As a reader of this book, you could be in any number of domestic situations. If you are a dyed-in-the-wool single person, then you will almost certainly find enough evidence in these pages to confirm you've made the right decision. If you already live with someone, then I'm sure that reading this book will encourage you to stick at it, knowing that you are not alone – other people have to put up with duvet stealers, eavesdroppers, phone hoggers and elephantine snorers too.

If you are about to take the plunge into couple-dom then CONGRATULATIONS!! Now buy this book – you'll need it.

Moving in with your partner is a huge decision. There are many different reasons why people give up their single life and embark on this path.

Maybe you've finally been kicked out of the family nest.

Perhaps it's the only way to stay in the country.

Maybe your dog died.

Maybe you found yourself drooling over a naked shop mannequin and then shamefully realised it didn't even have a head.

Maybe you got fed up with the checkout girl sniggering as you passed through your Friday night shopping basket, complete with its 'McCain's Ready-made Roast Dinner for One' that screams, 'another fun-packed weekend for me', and in a fit of desperation grabbed the nearest bag of bones with a pulse and said, 'Oh bugger, you'll do.'

Maybe you've fallen in love.

Who knows? Only one thing is for sure. From now on things around here are going to CHANGE.

In the coming weeks, months, years and decades (that's right, *decades*) you and your partner will learn many interesting and exciting things about each other. You will be intoxicated by new sights (oh dear), sounds (oh dear, oh dear) and smells (oh dear, oh dear, oh dear) that have hitherto been kept from you during the rosy honeymoon period that is NOW OVER.

With a bit of luck, your newly revealed habit of removing all your clothes before phoning your mum, and her insistence on sleeping with that special pillow (the one she's been sucking on since she was four, that's now the colour and smell of cat urine), will come as cute and fascinating surprises for you both to share and enjoy.

If you are a man, your friends can expect to see changes in you, as you shake off the last vestiges of your single life.

Your clothes will become cleaner, trendier and perhaps more beige. Your stomach will become larger, your wallet thinner. You will find yourself having to feel your way around the house, as perfectly good electric lights are dispensed with for more 'romantic' candles. Your parents will notice your gifts have become more thoughtful, and better wrapped.

If you are a woman, you can bask in the glory of being responsible for this 'miracle'. However, you may also find yourself wondering if the acquisition of a few extra oversized men's jumpers is enough to compensate you for losing your rights to the TV remote control.

This book aims to assist in smoothing the sometimes-painful transition from happy-go-lucky singleness to blissful couple-dom. I have tried to strike a good male–female balance but ultimately, this book is written from a man's perspective. This is for two reasons: One – I am a man (despite what you might think when you look at the photo on the front cover). Two – a man who claims to know what women think doesn't get laid, and I'm not stupid.

I hope this book helps you. You have a lot to look forward to. May you continue to grow 'in love and light'. Thank you for letting me make a difference to your life. Please excuse me now, my girlfriend needs a hand folding the bed sheets. Coming, dear. I'll just get the candles.

Jeff Green

The A–Z of
Living Together

A

Alcohol (*see also* Crying, Arguments, Losing things)

One of the most distressing discoveries in any new relationship is finding the woman you love and respect crumpled over the toilet bowl, dress riding up her back, exposing laddered tights and twisted gusset, one shoe missing, retching and breaking wind uncontrollably, demanding that you hold her hair out of her face and muttering something about having eaten a dodgy peanut. This is the power of alcohol. You, of course, never get *that* drunk.

> **TIP** In situations like these, it is always best to take photos for use in future negotiations, or for when these memories are met with denials (*see also* Flatulence).

Equally, there will be times when *your* basic abilities are impaired by alcohol. Attempting sex in this state is like trying to play snooker with a piece of rope. Don't be fooled by your partner's apparent compassion for your (hopefully) temporary predicament. News of this incident will be leaked to her friends at the earliest convenience. You may also find that, during moments of tension, you've acquired the nickname 'Mr Floppy'.

Anecdotes

We all like to exaggerate stories to make our lives seem a little bit more interesting, right? Why say you were travelling at 20 mph when the car skidded slightly, when you can say you were doing 60, had to avoid oncoming traffic, wrestled to keep control of the vehicle and are lucky to be sitting where you are now and not on a life-support machine, being played get well messages from your favourite band? No one gets hurt, you look like an exciting man of adventure, and you've brought a small amount of vicarious excitement into your guests' lives.

What's wrong with that? It's all part of being a man, right? The alternative is to do something genuinely brave and interesting, which is too silly to contemplate.

Of course, nothing is wrong with this, except that because you are now part of a couple, you will have the 'voice of truth' by your side (*see also* **Eavesdropping**), ready to pour iced water on to your fine skills as a raconteur:

YOU: So I managed to control the skid by giving it the opposite lock . . .
SHE: Oh, he talks such bollocks!

YOU: Excuse me?

SHE: It wasn't 60, it was more like 15, and we didn't skid at all.

YOU: Do I know you?

TIP 1 In social situations, always agree on which facts you are going to make up *before* arriving at the dinner party. This saves any unpleasantness in the car later.

TIP 2 At important work functions, you should ask your partner to avoid any anecdotes which include the following conversational gambits:
- Tell them about your run in with the police at your last job.
- Anyone else into bondage?
- Are you allowed to drink alcohol with cystitis?

Apologising

Say you're sorry. No one says you have to mean it.

TIP It's always a good idea to say sorry as soon as you wake up, in case you did something wrong in her dreams.

Arguments

Arguments can be fun. Some couples even see them as a form of communication, and relish the thought of their next little 'chat'. However, if you are one of those people who hate confrontation, don't worry. With the ready availability of **alcohol**, this needn't be a barrier.

If you intend to argue in public (and why not, most couples do), there are one or two things you can do to minimise disruption. In particular, learn to talk out the side of your mouth. This is very useful for arguing at dinner parties without being noticed:

At the dinner table

SHE: I've got my eye on you; you're drinking too much.

YOU: What?

SHE: You heard me. Slow it down.

YOU: I'll drink as much as I like.

SHE: You can't handle it.

YOU: Why don't you shut your trap?

SHE: You lousy bastard, you've ruined my life.

YOU: Not now.

SHE: I should have listened to my mother, she warned me about you.

YOU: Your mother's an old sow.

SHE: She's more of a man than you'll ever be!

YOU: Right, that's it. Get your coat.

Or in the kitchen

YOU: Having a good time, are we?

SHE: He's sixteen and the host's nephew, before you say anything.

YOU: Just let me know when you've finished making a fool of yourself.

SHE: Just let *me* know when *you've* finished being a pompous prat.

YOU: You lousy tart, you've ruined my life.

SHE: Not now.

YOU: My father warned me about you.

SHE: Your father was more of a man than *you'll* ever be.

YOU: Eh, what do you mean?

SHE: Never mind. Get your coat.

TIP 1 Remember, with any argument you're in it for the long haul. If you are not prepared to stay up for at least forty-eight hours without food and sleep, then you might as well concede your point straight away and retire hurt with your credit card to Agent Provocateur.

TIP 2 Late-night arguments can be won simply by threatening to walk to your mother's house, barefoot and penniless, in your nightdress.

B

Babies

Ways for you and your partner to avoid becoming broody: get up every hour throughout the night and burn £200.

Bad habits

We've all got one or two or thirty habits that we've become attached to over the years: nail-biting; scrotum-scratching; bum-picking; hair-sucking; maybe even a little earwax-snacking on the side. They're harmless activities that have given us hours of pleasure as we sit alone, blowing saliva bubbles, wondering why our relationships never last more than one date. However, as your domestic circumstances have now changed, you may think about reining in some of these pastimes a little for the good of the long-term partnership.

When is a habit bad?

It's all a matter of opinion but as a general rule, if pursuing the activity makes those nearby want to stab you, then it's probably considered 'bad'.

Bathrooms

You will have to accept very quickly that the bathroom no longer belongs to you (*see* **Personal space**). You are a mere visitor, and like all good visitors you will be expected to leave it in the same state you would want to find it. This will be difficult if you're one of those men who visit the loo during the night and urinate in the dark, using only their sense of hearing to locate the correct position to aim.

> **TIP** When peeing by 'sound' remember: Water on water – Good. Water on tile – Bad. Water on pyjama – V. Bad. Water on expensive face flannel she got from Harvey Nichols – V. V. Bad.

The Great Toilet Seat Debate

Some women accuse men of being thoughtless for leaving the toilet seat up. The truth of the matter is, men *do* try to pee with the seat down, but it causes such a mess it has to be put up to drain.

Baths

We all like a bath, right? It's a great way to get clean and can be quite relaxing. We don't need to sit in it for a fortnight, surrounded by candles, until we look like we're covered in the same skin Mother Nature used to create our scrotum, do we? Well apparently some of us (females) do.

> **TIP** Before getting in a bath always check the temperature of the water. It's a medical fact that women can tolerate much hotter water than men. They usually like it the temperature of lava, or at least to the point where you can light a cigarette off it.

Is your bath water too hot?
- Your foot looks like it's wearing a red popsock when you take it out.
- You get that weird sensation in your foot where you can't work out if the temperature is too hot or too cold.
- Your partner thinks it's a little on the 'tepid' side.

Bills (*see also* Lies, Arguments, The telephone, etc.)

Ideally, these should be paid out of that bank account you both set up that never has any money in it.

Bin-bagged

Colloquial term for when you've been thrown out of the house (probably due to some misunderstanding about what constitutes 'coming home straight away'), and all your belongings are lying on the pavement in black plastic refuse sacks. As in, 'Mum. (*Sniff.*) Is my old room still free? I've been bin-bagged.'

Blame – *see* Making decisions together

Bonding (*see also* Acts of subjugation)

You will find that some things are done not from necessity, but because they are considered to have a deeper meaning, or because they create bonds that lead to greater intimacy.

Letting your partner pee in front of you – right or wrong?

If you have a combined toilet and bathroom, your partner may, occasionally, ask to have a pee while you're cleaning your teeth at bedtime (or any other time while you're in there – to be honest, they're not fussy). If you agree to this, it will signify to her that you share a higher love that is only achieved between two adults prepared to forgo normal etiquette. I say, let it happen, but don't be alarmed when she says she just needs a 'tinkle' and then makes a sound like an elephant jet-washing a milk-tanker.

Boredom

Inevitably, there will come a day when you're picking the yellow fungus off your feet, and she's plucking her moustache line, and you'll both think, 'I do believe this relationship has lost a bit of its pizzazz.'

Has your relationship become lacklustre? Try this simple test:

- During lovemaking, you stop to ask if she's okay because she moved. (10 pts)
- You both look forward to Monday mornings. (15 pts)
- You buy Horlicks in catering packs. (15 pts)
- Even she can't remember what she just said. (20 pts)

How to tackle boredom – do's and don'ts

- Do – Buy her some sexy underwear, such as a G-string. Then for an extra special night, ask her to wear it back to front. Grrrrrr!
- Don't – Suggest a threesome with her sister or best friend. (No matter how well you all seem to be getting on when you're drunk.)
- Do – Go for long walks in the park. Then, if you both like it, try going together.
- Do – Suggest sex in the car. (But not if it's a two-seater sports car, unless you're a qualified osteopath, double-jointed, or dating a midget.)

Bringing friends back from the pub

Your friends:

YOU: (*poking head round the door*) I've brought some friends back from the pub. Okay?

SHE: (*in T-shirt and pants, painting toenails by the fire, suddenly alarmed*) What?

YOU: Just some friends.

SHE: What friends?

YOU: Erm, new friends.

SHE: New friends? You mean strangers? No way.

YOU: Oh, come on love. They're all right. They just need a place to stay till the police release their convoy in the morning.

SHE: GET THEM OUT!

YOU: (*in hallway*) Sorry guys, no can do. She's fast asleep.

Her friends:

SHE: (*bursting through door, falling backwards on to couch and shouting*) I'm home.

YOU: (*in underpants, eating Weetabix, watching TV*) So I see.

SHE: Shut up and give us a kiss, you boring bastard.

YOU: I'm watching telly.

SHE: (*not listening*) My feet are bloody killing me. (*She kicks her shoes off – one of them lands in the fire, the other in your cereal bowl.*) That's better. Do my feet stink?

(*Sound of front door kicked open, bottles clanking and very loud cackling and swearing from the hallway.*)

SHE: (*over her shoulder*) In here girls. The girls have come back for a quick drink. You don't mind do you?

YOU: (*wiping milk off your face*) Not at all. The company of drunk women is always a delight.

SHE: Well tough. (*Pause.*) Oh.

Burping

I'm sorry to say that although much prized and admired, the fabulous and immensely gratifying art of making a belch last as long as possible has no place in modern dining. Therefore you must ask her to desist from doing it.

C

Candles

Remember when these were just for birthdays and when the miners went on strike? Well not any more. For some reason, women love candles (could they have some moth genes in them?). Apparently, they're 'romantic', they make the place 'nice and cosy', and they hide untidiness (now you're talking). So I'm afraid from now on you'll just have to get used to bashing your shins against coffee tables, putting out small domestic fires, not having a clue what you're eating, and discovering your partner in the bath, looking as if she's ready to contact the dead.

TIP To avoid unpleasant bumps and scrapes during periods of reduced visibility, why not install aeroplane-style floor lighting in your home to help guide you to the kitchen, bedroom and bathroom?

Cats

The simple rule is, like exclamation marks, more than two signifies complete nutcase.

Change (coins)

Remember when you used to keep all your loose change in a jar by the bed to be rifled later for emergency bus fares and cartons of milk? Well, the bad news is, you've been spotted. Now that little jar of yours has become 'our jar' (*see also* '**Our stuff**'):

YOU: Where've all the pound coins gone from my jar?

SHE: What jar?

YOU: What do you mean – *what jar*? The jar I see you with your hand in every morning, like Winnie the Pooh.

SHE: The money jar?

YOU: Yes, the money jar. Or rather, *my* money jar.

SHE: I've been throwing coins in there too.

YOU: When?

SHE: All the time.

YOU: I've never seen you.

SHE: Well I have.

YOU: When was the last time?

SHE: I can't remember.

YOU: Oh you must. Think back, who was Prime Minister?

SHE: Don't be cheap. It isn't attractive.

YOU: You're right. Can you lend me a pound?

SHE: (generously) Have a look in my jar.

Charm offensive

There will be times when you screw up so badly that the very survival of your relationship will be thrown into doubt. Such occasions may include:

- Forgetting to videotape her favourite soap, after promising on your life to do it.
- Taping her favourite soap, but using her university graduation video to do so.
- Accidentally leaving your dirty underpants skiddy side up in the bathroom when her boss comes round for drinks.
- Shouting your ex's/her best friend's/your best friend's/ her mum's/the dog's name upon orgasm.

In such circumstances you will have to go on an immediate and full scale **charm offensive** to worm your way back into her affections.

Consider the following:

- Put toilet seat down (okay, even if wet).
- Show interest in story lines/characters from those favourite soaps. (But don't point at Barbara Windsor and say, 'Blimey, Sharon's let herself go.')
- Light the house as if celebrating a very old person's birthday.

- Give her a relaxing massage (warning: giving her a ten-second arm tickle then saying 'Now you do me' won't work).
- Offer unsolicited compliments about:
    Her hair (will need to be more than 'I like you with hair')
    Her eyes ('Hmm, two eyes . . . lovely')
    Her bum ('Nice crack')
- Tell her how amazing her friends think she is:

YOU: Your friends think you're great.

SHE: They do not.

YOU: They do.

SHE: Don't be silly.

YOU: Honestly, I can see it, they really *admire* you.

SHE: (*feigning disinterest*) I don't believe you. Which friends?

YOU: All of them.

SHE: (*silence, except for the sound of cat lapping up milk*)

Choice

Something you both took for granted before you decided to live with another person (*see also* **Opinions**).

Chores (*see also* Washing-up, Holding hands, Removing socks before sex, etc.)

Sadly, the days of our fathers, when men were not expected to do anything around the house except sit in a comfy chair drinking tea and Brown Ale and threatening the children, are long gone. Nowadays you will be expected to do your bit. However, don't panic:

Ways to avoid chores:
- Drop into the conversation that the woman who runs the launderette is really good looking, and that you think it's a shame she's obviously single and lonely. This should put a stop to you being sent *there* again.
- Put the cat on your chest, concuss it, then say, 'I can't do the washing-up, the cat's asleep on me.'
- When your partner pulls up with a car full of shopping, snort some Amyl Nitrate and then tell her you're having a heart attack.

Clichés

The following clichés have been used in the making of this book:

Women cry a lot

Men make lists

Men tug themselves off in the shed

Women like kissing and cuddling

Men hog the remote control

Women are always cold

Men are messy

Men are mean

Women buy lots of shoes and lie about the cost

Women need lots of reassurance

Clothes – *see* 'Our stuff'

Comfort (*see also* Duvets, Candles, Electric blankets, Heating, etc., etc.)

Why is your partner so obsessed with comfort when she gets home? Hard to say. It could be genetic, or it could be because she spends the whole day wearing dodgy shoes and knickers that go so far up the crack of her bum she feels like she's being constantly thrown out of a nightclub.

Commitment (*see also* Bonding)

Signs she will interpret as you showing commitment to her:

- Assigning a special button to her favourite radio station on the car stereo.
- Changing the answerphone message from: '*I'm* not in' to '*We're* not in'.
- Signing family Christmas cards from you both.
- Giving her the pink brush attachment of your electric toothbrush.

Signs you interpret as her showing commitment:

- Swallowing.

That pretty much covers it.

Compliments

We all like a compliment. It can brighten our day. To keep your relationship healthy and happy, you should compliment your partner freely. However, the following are not considered compliments:

- You are a fantastic cleaner.
- Wow. You can trough your food down, can't you?
- What amazing breasts. I'll bet they keep your knees nice and warm in winter.
- You remind me of my mum.

Your partner may also care to rethink saying the following:

- At least your back hair isn't receding.
- Hey, small is beautiful.
- I wish I had your legs.
- You remind me of my dog.

Compromise

Or, to put it another way, 'let's neither of us have any fun'.

What is a compromise? A shabby back-room deal, reached when the usual avenues of emotional blackmail, crying, threats to walk out, tantrums and sulking fail to work.

Do compromises work? Have you ever tasted Rosé?

Contraception

These days, of course, responsibility must be shared. So it follows that if *you* bought the condom and *you* wore it, then it's *her* job to get rid of it before *you* tread on it barefoot later.

Cooking

One of the great benefits of living with someone is the extra mouth they bring to the dinner table, thus releasing you from the sad, single person tedium of having to eat the same meal (I'm getting a strong image of Spaghetti Bolognese here) for the next three weeks.

Of course, like men and **DIY**, it is a myth that women possess an innate ability to cook. Some have been known to look up the recipe for toast. However it is true that all women know how to make those Rice Krispie chocolate crackle cakes. (They're taught in school, you know.) For me, the fact that they choose not to make them every day, hints at a darker side.

It must be remembered that cooking is a difficult skill, which requires patience and confidence. Enthusiasm is easily dampened if you say the wrong thing. So when you or your partner appraise the other's newly developed cooking skills, be careful not to say:

- My god, did you drop it?
- Great, ratatouille (unless you've been told that's what it is).

- Don't worry, I know a good restaurant that delivers.
- Sorry, I've just eaten.
- Why don't you just serve it in the dog's bowl and cut out the middleman?

TIP When serving leftovers to friends, disguise the fact by calling it 'Tapas'.

Crying

Remember, love is like a garden. It needs to be watered regularly. With tears. (*See also* **Arguments**, **DIY**, **Charm offensive**.)

Of course, as well as being an indication of pain and hurt, crying is also an awesomely powerful tool for **getting what you want**. Some women (and male politicians) have known this for millennia; it's a secret that gets handed down from mother to daughter through the generations, along with how to remove a bra without taking your T-shirt off on the beach, and how to get a towel to stay on your head after you've washed your hair.

The fact is there is nothing stopping you from using a few tears yourself in order to swing things to your advantage. For example, if you forget to purchase a gift for her birthday, why not burst into tears the moment she challenges you:

SHE: (*upset*) It's my birthday today. You haven't bought me a present or even a card. That's so rotten of you. What's going on?

YOU: I know darling. What can I say? I'm such a failure. (*Cry Now!*)

SHE: Hey, hey. Where's all this come from?

YOU: (*Sobbing uncontrollably*) I'm sorry, I'm so sorry. I'm so, so sorry. (*Okay, don't overdo it.*) I'm such a crap boyfriend. I don't deserve you.

SHE: (*Disturbed.*) Come on now. Where's all this come from? It's not so bad. It's only a silly birthday.

YOU: (*More waterworks.*)

SHE: Hey, I've got an idea. Why don't I buy *you* a little present?

YOU: (*sniffle*) If you really want to.

SHE: Of course. I'd love to.

YOU: I'd quite like a car.

Cuddling

Pleasant act of affection always requested at the wrong time.

Cute

With a bit of luck, this is what your girlfriend thinks you are. A lot of men rely on this to save them when they are in big trouble (*see* **Charm offensive**). Remember though, cute doesn't last forever (*see* **Jimmy Osmond, Jason Donovan**, etc.)

Protect your cuteness. Try to avoid:

- Dancing with your underpants pulled high up to your chest at her office party.
- Breaking wind in the bath and then saying: 'Did you just hear Bill and Ben say something?'
- Pushing your genitals between your legs and strutting around the bedroom declaring, 'Look love, I'm a girl too!'

D

Decorating

There are some very reasonably priced painters and deco-
rators in the phone book, as well as some expensive
relationship counsellors. The choice is yours.

Dieting

It is highly likely that cohabitation will result in you both
putting on a few dozen pounds in the first year (no doubt
due to all that take-away food – *see* **Cooking**). In fact,
unless you're a Breatharian who has moved in with a
supermodel, living up-close and personal with your partner will show you the shocking reality of just how much
nosh you both can put away in a twenty-four-hour period.
If you're not hearing her say, 'I'm starving,' she's probably
saying, 'That was lovely.' If this is the case, then at some
point you may both decide that you need to embark on a
diet.

TIP 1 Secretly buy a pair of trousers two sizes too big, and then when someone asks how the diet's going, pull out the waistband and say, 'Great. I've lost this much all ready.'

TIP 2 When purchasing exercise equipment, make sure it is of sturdy construction and that there is enough space to hang all your wet washing on it.

Discharges

HERS: Caused by an uncomfortable yeast infection. Can be cured with natural yoghurt.

YOURS: Caused by strange night-thoughts that give you a funny feeling in your doodle. Who wants a cure?

DIY

Here, the rule seems to be, expect plenty of demands but very little practical support when it comes to doing those little jobs around the home. Most men are quite poor at DIY. This is mainly because they were only trusted to make a wooden fish in school carpentry lessons. So when a woman asks, 'Can you put some shelves up?' most men will automatically respond with, 'Sure, cod or halibut?'

Tools

Some women possess excellent tool kits. Others will hand you a set of miniature screwdrivers they got out of a Christmas cracker and say, 'Can you fix the washing machine, please?'

TIP 1 Beware falling for the flannel that 'seeing a man performing DIY is sexy'. Soon it'll be 'Watching a guy ironing really gets me horny' and 'When a man hands over large amounts of crisp cash, god, that makes me hot'.

TIP 2 Avoid the temptation to put a mirror on the bedroom ceiling. Not only will you be unable to cope with the shocking truth about her love handles and your bum hair (or indeed your love handles and her bum hair), but also ask yourself this – is it wise to suspend a large piece of plate glass over your sleeping face when it's a well-known fact that superglue isn't what it used to be?

Duvets

They say women are the weaker sex, but have you ever tried to get the duvet off her at four o'clock in the morning?

E

Earplugs

You may notice that your sense of when an argument is over can differ from hers by several days (*see also* **Twenty questions**). During such times, earplugs can be lifesavers. Do remember to paint them flesh coloured and to say randomly, 'Well can't you video yourself at another graduation?' to avoid detection.

Of course it is equally possible that your partner may wish to slip a pair in whenever you decide to give her the unexpurgated biographies of the peripheral members of AC/DC, when telling her the differences and long-term cost benefits of using super-unleaded petrol instead of plain unleaded, or when giving her the great news about Global Satellite Positioning (*see also* **Boredom, Selective hearing**).

Eavesdropping

You'd better get used to it, you will have your conversations snooped on. But before you jump up and start shouting about invasion of privacy, think how she would feel if she found out about your little visits to her under-wear drawer.

Do women listen in on private telephone conversations? Try this simple test:

Sit with the phone at your ear and affect having a normal telephone conversation. Now, with one eye on your partner, say one of the following and see if you observe a reaction:

- Well, how about you all come over?
- So how's Sally with the big boobs?
- Really, they're giving away free kittens?

Electric blankets

Magnificent inventions and I heartily recommend you get one. It'll certainly stop that subterfuge of needing a cuddle because the bed's 'like an Eskimo's nose'.

> **TIP** If, god forbid, you have forgotten to turn on the electric blanket and it's −6°C in the bedroom, a good emergency 'fix' is the 'flossing ruse'. Insist that tonight's the night to start your new flossing regime. Then slowly pick away at your teeth, making sure she has to enter the icy bed first. Don't forget to climb in on the side she's just warmed up, too. 'Come on love, move along.' Bliss.

Excuses

Emergency excuses/actions for all occasions:

- Forgetting to water the houseplants – Can't you see? I let them die because I thought you loved them more than you loved me. (Especially effective if you can do it through hacking sobs – *see* **Crying**.)
- Being caught looking at porn on the Internet – Can you believe that? Someone has hacked into the Salvation Army website and put rude pictures up.
- Forgetting to buy a birthday card – Make a card quickly out of scrap paper. Draw a childish flower on the front and write 'Happy Birthday' on the inside. Then give it saying, 'Any idiot can buy a card from a shop but it takes a special kind of love to make one for you.'

Exes – Where to hide the videos?

It has to be somewhere she never goes – how about the shoe polish box? Or simply mark them 'Nude Gardening with Alan Titchmarsh'.

Extracting extra credit for small acts of thoughtfulness

It's possible that your spontaneous acts of kindness and consideration will be few and far between. It is therefore important that each one you manage is fully noticed, remembered for eternity and accrues you the largest possible return benefit. For this to be achieved you must not be afraid to keep banging on about each and every small gift you have proffered till the words gag at the back of your throat:

YOU: Wake up love.
SHE: What is it? Are we in danger?
YOU: Remember that Kit-Kat I gave you last February?
SHE: Oh not again. It's four a.m.
YOU: Wasn't that nice of me?
SHE: Yes. Why are you doing this to me?
YOU: Just thought I'd mention it. Night, night.

F

Fears

It is a sad fact that by falling in love you have presented yourself as a hostage to fortune. You will lie awake at night when your loved one isn't home at the agreed time, worrying that she may be having a bad time. In the same way, when you're not home on time, she will lie awake worrying that you're having a good time.

Feng Shui

Ancient Chinese art of getting men to put the toilet lid down.

Flatulence

Do women fart? If you are of a nervous disposition and do not wish to know the answer to this question please skip the next page. . .

OH YES.

Flirting (*see also* Having an affair)

It's probably best not to do this too much, as most mortgages incur large penalties for early cancellations.

Foot odour

Smelly feet are not big or clever, and very rarely funny, although to be fair, a malodorous walking shoe held closely to a sleeping nose can brighten any camping trip.

Do women's feet smell? *See* **Flatulence**.

Forgiveness – something to try once

Of course some things are unforgivable:
- Drinking the last of the milk before bed.
- Standing in front of the TV during a penalty shootout, demanding you help fold the bed sheets.
- Using her best eyeliner as an emergency pencil. Apparently.
- Stealing your chewing gum during a kiss.
- Eating both After Eight mints at the curry house while you're away in the loo.
- Putting cigarettes out in an unfinished can of beer. And then not mentioning it.

Friends – so important in times of conflict

It's understandable if you feel slightly envious of the close relationship your partner shares with her friends. In times of crisis, such as a break up, they offer a strong support structure that involves as many of them as possible coming round, getting drunk and calling you a feckless prick. You, on the other hand, will be lucky to rustle up one pal, even sadder than you, who will proceed to 'help' by telling you how great your partner was, how you'll never find anyone as good as her, the extraordinary length of time you can expect to be on your own (forever) and could he possibly have her phone number, as he'd like to give her a call while she's feeling confused and vulnerable.

Furniture

Perhaps the most significant item of furniture in any relationship is of course the couch. This is where battles will be won and lost, victories celebrated, take-away food consumed and children conceived.

Important considerations when buying a couch:
- In years to come will it provide us with a small income from monies recovered from down the back?
- Is it big enough to sleep on during times of tension/snoring/flu/Hugh Grant films?
- Is it large enough to discourage opportunistic cuddling during important TV sports moments?

- Is it tough enough to stand excessive jumping up and down upon during important TV sports moments?
- Can it accommodate two people without touching when those two people have had a row and are trying to out-sulk each other?
- Are the covers machine-washable for when those same two people have just made up?

G

Gardening

The fact that some people can gain pleasure from what is in effect nothing more than self-imposed community service remains a mystery.

> **TIP** Avoid garden centres. There is nothing more depressing than being dragged around one on a Sunday morning – especially if you don't even have a garden.

Genital warts

Unfortunate affliction caused by having sex with toads. Can be removed with modern cryogenics or simply left alone – the resultant sexual sensation can't be too dissimilar from that obtained from a novelty condom.

Getting what you want (*see also* Compromise)

There are many ways for you and your partner to bend each other to your will (*see also* **Crying, Tantrums, Grovelling, Gifts, Oral sex**).

For Her: Emotional blackmail
'Don't worry about picking me up if you're too busy watching TV, I can walk home alone – I know a short cut through Flasher's Alley.'

For Him: Sulking
SHE: It's like going out with a child.
(*Silence*)
SHE: Look, you haven't said anything for three days, when is it going to end?
(*Silence*)
SHE: Okay, you can have the sweets out the middle but you've got to save the chocolate egg till Sunday.
YOU: Thanks love. I knew you'd see it my way.

Gifts

To keep your relationship running smoothly you will need to oil it regularly. The preferred lubricant is love and affection, but failing that gifts and compliments are a useful substitute.

Warning. *The following are not considered gifts:*

- Diet books
- Cooking utensils
- Cleaning products
- Petrol for the car
- Anything from the Pound shop

'Giving is better than receiving'

Popular expression used to encourage especially mean and ungrateful people (*see* **Dads** and **Teenagers** – sorry, wrong book) into gift-giving. Can also be applied to anal sex.

Grinding teeth – *see* Sleeping and Grounds for murder

Grovelling

Much underrated method of obtaining sex in the event that **charm offensive** doesn't work.

Guilt (*see also* Gym membership)

Pointless, negative emotion that is easily removed by a simple lowering of basic personal standards.

H

Hair

Let's face it, if you live with a woman you're going to have to get used to coming into contact with hair. Huge clumps of it. Wrapped around stuff. Enough to weave a welcome mat with change for a luxuriant murkin.

Frankly, women have more hair than men and they are not afraid to lose it. By all accounts, from the amount collected from the plughole and wrapped around your toothbrush, your partner should be bald.

Questions worth asking your partner after a visit to the bathroom:
- Are you taking a bath wearing a mohair jumper?
- Are you operating a pet-grooming business from the premises?
- Are there any longhaired guinea pigs in your ancestry?

Hair bands

If your partner's hair is longer than shoulder length then you will start to find vast numbers of these elasticised hair ties around the home. Note I said 'you', because she can never find one. That's why she buys more. Soon they'll be turning up everywhere: in the bed, on door handles, cutting off the blood supply to your big toe. They are not even very good for flicking at her arse in an immature fashion.

> **NOTE** It is possible that, like an animal 'scenting' its patch, so the hair band, sanitary towel wrapper and make-up caked cotton ball are female territory-markers that say to other females, 'This is my space – kindly vacate the area as a stiletto to the head often offends.'

Handkerchiefs – *see* Toilet paper

Hangovers

Two people rattling around a house nursing large hangovers (although it is possible that yours is a brain tumour that's been misdiagnosed) will provide endless possibilities for interpersonal hostilities. I suggest one of you leaves the country until they pass.

Happiness – *see* Love and Alcohol

Having an affair (*see also* Flirting with your clothes off, etc.)

You don't need me to tell you that this is seriously dodgy behaviour. If you insist on having an affair, then you must plan ahead. Very often, men like you are caught out because of sudden changes in appearance and behaviour. One day paisley nylon underpants and a quick squirt of 'Haze' under the pits before perfunctory copulation, next golden lycra posing pouch, all-over 'Kouros' body swill, and then into some strange continental-style sexual shenanigans, like foreplay. How did she know?

Starting from *now*, you must affect a secretive manner – when your mum phones say, 'I think I'll just take it in the shed', ceremonially burn all your receipts, start wearing large amounts of flashy jewellery when visiting elderly relatives, and learn how to go pale to the sound of the doorbell ringing. You must also start coming home from work at five a.m. every night.

You might consider 'confessing' to mild transvestism early on in your relationship when these things are more easily forgiven. Years later, when you are discovered with lipstick on your clothes and naff underwear in your car, you can both laugh it off as that little peculiarity of yours.

TIP Keep a diary of all those clandestine meetings so that when you've been caught and thrown out (*see* **Bin-bagged**), and you're living in a homeless drop-in centre in Rotherham, spending your days introducing people at cash machines to the tangy aroma of urine-soaked clothing and only getting to see the kids for trips to the zoo, at least you'll have some memories of why it was all worth it.

Do women have affairs? *See* **Flatulence**.

Heating

Women love having the central heating on in the home. They start sneaking it on around July just in case a possible 'cold snap' catches them out in August.

Tell-tale signs someone (female) has been interfering with the heating controls:

- You're watching TV from the fridge in your underpants.
- You notice your weight is down to four stone and your shoes are melting.
- The cat is demanding to be shaved.
- The local botanical gardens ask if they can store their tropical Brazilian collection with you.

Hobbies

If you live in one of our bigger cities you probably only have one, and that's getting home from work in one piece.

Holding hands

When you start living together, your life changes. You may find it difficult to adjust to being hassled – sorry, wrong word – *loved* twenty-four hours a day. However, there is nothing more delightful than walking through the park hand in hand with your loved one.

Inappropriate occasions for holding hands:
- Riding a bicycle
- Washing-up
- Whilst using adjacent gym treadmills
- Swimming
- On the lavatory
- Approaching a roundabout at 50 mph

'Home alone'

Unless you're one of those unfortunate souls who can't bear to be away from your loved one, time left alone while your partner visits family and friends will become much prized. In fact, why not take a leaf out of women's books and use the time to really pamper yourself. Dress for dinner – vest and underpants. Take time to make the place just how *you* want it – like it's been burgled. Ten minutes should do it. Eat your meals in stages: beans first, pie later, potatoes for breakfast. Drink milk straight out of the carton. Leave every light on in the house. To round it off, how about sleeping in the car? Luxury.

Honesty

By far the most important element in any relationship and thus must be used sparingly, to save it from becoming mundane.

Honeymoon period

Telltale signs that it's over:
- Her bra and knickers stop matching.
- She asks you to pick up her Anusol prescription from the chemist on your way home.
- You no longer take your socks off before having sex.
- She no longer takes her tights off before having sex.

Illness (*see also* Hangovers)

One of the major perks of living with someone who thinks they love you is the opportunity it gives for copious amounts of indulged hypochondria. What better way to spend a week than being spoon-fed home-made soup and having your pillows fluffed up when secretly you know the only thing wrong with you is eye strain from reading magazines, mild Lucozade sickness and a slight headache from too many *Countdown* conundrums.

> **TIP** Secretly purchase a medical dictionary. One read should give you all the necessary psychosomatic symptoms for a lifetime's loafing. Failing that, try these good non-detectable staples:
>
> *Back pain.* External symptoms – None. Cure – Plenty of horizontal rest and definitely no lifting.
>
> *Grumbling appendix.* Symptoms – Non-specific stomach pains (just hold the right side of your stomach and groan a bit). Cure – I'm afraid you're just going to have to put up with being inactive for a few days.

Migraine. Symptoms – Very bad headache (just hold your head and groan a bit). Cure – Lie down in a darkened room until it passes. May take several hours. Or until something good comes on the telly.

Acute halitosis – I only mention this because I can't imagine anyone wanting to check.

'I'm not angry, I'm disappointed.'

Hurrah!

Insults

Sometimes reason and thought have to take a back seat. In such situations you will need the biggest, fattest, cruellest, juiciest insult to let them know that this time, they've pushed you too far.

Emergency insults for every occasion:
- Oh yeah? Well when God gave you teeth he spoiled a bloody good arse!
- Thanks a lot, baby. You made me feel as welcome as a hang-glider with diarrhoea.
- Nice try, sweetheart. You know, with a little practice you could be really unpleasant.
- Well, you smell. (My favourite.)

Intruders

It doesn't always have to be your turn to check. All you have to do is surrender a little dignity:

SHE: I heard a noise.

YOU: Sorry about that, I thought you were asleep.

SHE: No, a proper noise. Downstairs. Did you hear it?

YOU: (*lying*) No.

SHE: You must have.

YOU: Afraid not. I had my fingers in my ears.

SHE: Go and see what it is.

YOU: I can't, my legs have been chopped off.

SHE: What?

YOU: I didn't want to tell you. It happened earlier.

SHE: You're supposed to protect me.

YOU: In the old days, maybe, but society has moved on. I don't make the rules. Are you enjoying the vote?

SHE: I thought you were tough.

YOU: No way. I haven't had a fight since I was eleven and I only won that because she had an asthma attack.

SHE: I never knew I was living with a coward.

YOU: Well, you live and learn. Now move over and sleep nearest to the door.

'I *told* you' (*see also* Selective hearing)

If you're in the habit of only listening to ten per cent of what your girlfriend says then statistically you will, *eventually*, miss something worth hearing. So don't expect any sympathy if at some point in the not-too-distant future she arrives back with her parents to find you in the lounge, halfway through an act of pleasurable self-abuse. You have been warned.

J

Jealousy

This unfortunate 'illness' is a destructive force in relationships and should not be tolerated in any form. **Don't** be
annoyed with her when she talks to one of your friends for
too long before she hands the phone over. **Do** expect a
glass ashtray delivered swiftly to the side of your head if
you mention how sexy Meg Ryan looks in a movie.

Joint accounts (*see also* Bills)

It is always a good idea to set up a separate bank account
to pay for those essential communal items like Gucci
handbags, manicures, waxings and wine bills from All Bar
One.

Jokes

When has a joke gone too far? (*See* **Emergency services**.)

Journeys

No doubt there will be times when you both need a break from spending time together in the home. An enjoyable change is to go for a 'drive'. However, as well as bringing pleasure (for example – duetting at the top of your voices to 'I've Got You Babe' by Cher while weaving through oncoming traffic . . . just me then), the car also offers many areas for potential conflict (*see also* **Arguments, Self-defence in enclosed spaces, Nagging**). So before embarking on any car journey it is a good idea to agree upon a few basic rules:

1 Do not distract the driver by pointing out 'nice' things in shop windows.
2 No trying to sing 'properly'.
3 When borrowing the vehicle, do leave the driver's seat in the position it was found, i.e. not half an inch from the windscreen.
4 A squeegee merchant's slopping of the windscreen does not constitute a wash.
5 That money in the ashtray is for parking meters, not for magazines and cigarettes.
6 In the event of a breakdown, both able-bodied parties are at liberty to push.
7 Definitely no Sting or Alanis Morrisette! (Unless you are Sting or Alanis Morrisette.)

Jumpers – *see* 'Our stuff'

Juvenile behaviour

Term used to describe everything you do after you've upset her.

K

Kissing

In the early stages of your relationship, you will be expected to present your lips for kissing a few hundred times a day. Don't panic, this phase soon passes and should settle down to a more manageable couple of dozen after a few weeks. Later, it may even be possible to substitute less important kisses for the odd peck on the cheek, or ideally for the more practical handshake, for example when leaving the country on business, upon the birth of your first child, or indeed after sex.

TIP To avoid kissing, why not do what a lot of men do and grow a moustache?

Kitchen

The perfect place to make Rice Krispie chocolate crackles. Hint hint. (Let it go, Jeff.)

Knickers (*see also* G-strings, Honeymoon period, etc.)

Part of the fun of living with a woman, is discovering where a pair of her pants will be found next. Will it be behind the radiator, covered in fluff? Or maybe down the couch, wrapped inside a pair of tights? How about in one of your dressing-gown pockets? Or, just maybe, wedged down at the bottom of the bed between the sheets? Counting the pairs you find might even give you a good indication of how often you had sex that week/month/year.

Uses for old knickers
None. Look along the radiator – does it look like she ever throws any of them out?

Knick-knacks (aka mementoes)

You are both probably having trouble letting go of those favourite little possessions you've acquired over the years (*see also* **Exes' photos**). If you've got a couple of Oscars you could be forgiven for wanting to put them on public display. However, taking up the entire mantelpiece and all available shelf space with your Pub Pool trophies, school 5-metre breaststroke certificates and cycling proficiency badges might be overdoing it.

By the same token, *you* might argue that having to fight your way through several dozen one-eyed, stuffed furry 'friends' to get into bed every night can become a little wearing. How many times is getting Dumbo in a headlock and punching his lights out, or drop-kicking ET against the wardrobe doors, funny? Well, quite a few times actually, but there are limits.

So what to do with precious keepsakes? The safest bet is to gather them all up and put them in the attic ready for your grandchildren to ridicule one day.

TIP Don't be bullied into selling your sporting memorabilia at the local car boot sale. These items seldom raise the sums you expect and anyway, would you be comfortable knowing that there was some impostor out there getting laid on the presumption that it was *he* who was Division 3 Runner-up – West Hartlepool Pub League Darts Championship1987? I don't think so.

KY Jelly

If you run out when the chemist is closed, a fine emergency substitute is something called 'foreplay'. Failing this, try that substance you get in the middle of pork pies.

L

Laughter (see also Injuries, Smiling, etc.)

To keep love alive, every relationship should be sprinkled with liberal amounts of joyous laughter.

Occasions when it is best for you not to laugh
- When she models her new sexy underwear
- When she's giving birth
- When you win an argument
- When she stubs her toe on something she told you several times to put away
- When she tells you how she felt when her favourite pet died
- When she says she didn't reach orgasm
- Just after saying sorry
- When she tells you she thinks you two are soul mates

Occasions when it is best for her not to laugh

- When your team lose
- When she first sees your doodle

That pretty much covers it.

Laundry (*see also* Underpants)

Whoever said girls are made of 'sugar and spice' obviously never saw one sniffing the crotch of her tights in the morning to see if she can get another wear out of them.

> **TIP** It is universally acknowledged that not all laundry is 'dirty' *per se*. We have all been guilty of throwing some of our most favoured garments into the washing basket before they are strictly unwearable. On such occasions, you are perfectly entitled to 'rescue' these items from the basket when you have nothing else to wear. To save confusion when you are rushing to an important job interview/business meeting/romantic date and need to do a quick 'recycle', why not make a habit of organising dirty laundry in the following categories:
>
> Looks OK/Smells OK – Wear as normal
> Looks bad/Smells OK – Wear under a jumper
> Looks OK/Smells bad – Spray heavily with deodorant
> Looks bad/smells bad – Only go out at night and insist on a 'no hugs' rule

Leaving in a huff

It's a simple thing, but do remember to take everything with you when you storm out. There is nothing more embarrassing than having to re-enter the room you have just proudly left with an unrepeatable dramatic flourish:

YOU: Yeah? Well, when God gave you an arse he spoiled some bloody good teeth. No, that's not right. OK. Well, you smell! Goodbye forever. (*Slam.*)
PAUSE
(*Creaking door*)
(*Meekly*) Sorry. Forgot my inhaler. Bye love.

Lies

I'm sorry to break it to you but it's highly likely your partner is going to lie to you. In fact, if you've ever been told that the slinky black dress in the expensive shopping bag (with rope handles) was bought in error while she was looking for something for you, then it's probably already happened.

Some of the favourite lies we tell:
- I wouldn't bother turning over. I've looked in the TV guide and there's nothing on except this (which just happens to be my favourite programme)
- I looked for the cheaper pair but they'd sold out
- We don't have to stay long

- It was like that when I found it
- I had to finish them, they were going off
- He: Now you mention it, it *does* look smaller
- She: Now you mention it, it *does* look bigger
- ....[*Reader to add own here*]

Lipstick

Whether you like it or not, living with a woman means you will become acquainted with some of her female problems (*see also* **Yoghurt**, **Vaginal flatulence**, etc.). A minor, but tricky problem is lipstick on the teeth. At its worst, some women can end up looking like they've just finished sucking the blood out of a squirrel.

The best way to tell someone they have lipstick on their teeth is to just come out and say it. 'Excuse me, Miss, but I think your teeth are bleeding.' The trouble comes when you engage in complicated secret codes, like running your tongue over your own teeth, which can so easily be misconstrued. Especially if you are trying to inform a non-family member over the age of sixty, or a transvestite.

Losing things

Remember when you used to know where everything was? You dropped something on the floor and there it was, six weeks later, exactly how you left it except for a bit of green mould on the top. Remember when you could start a conversation with your loved one without using the words 'Have you seen . . .?' 'Where's my . . .?' and 'What the hell has happened to . . .?' Welcome to the world of Cohabitation.

NOTE It's one of those odd things that your partner will always know where your wallet is:

YOU: Have you seen my keys?

SHE: No. And anyway I'm not your mother. (*Then something really helpful like*) Where did you last have them?

YOU: In a lock. What about my wallet?

SHE: Upstairs. Second drawer down. Blue trousers, back pocket.

YOU: Amazing.

Losing keys – Drink being a factor

Losing your keys upon arriving home from a boys' night out is, of course, an altogether different proposition. You sober up very quickly, as the awful realisation sinks in that you are going to have to wake her up, and get her out of bed. (Is there a way of waking someone up without waking them up?) This is officially known as being 'in the shit'. (*Now see* **Charm offensive**.)

TIP The important phrase here is: 'I love you'. When calling through the letterbox every sentence must contain it at least once. As in:

(*Sound of creaky brass letterbox being pushed open.*
Letterbox springs back violently, catching drunken
fingers.)

YOU: (*barely whispered hiss*) Bugger. (*Sound of fingers*
being blown on by lips not in full communication
with brain.) Pherrrrrrrph. Pherrrrrrrph.
(*Letterbox pushed open more carefully this time.*
From upstairs, sound of child's recorder being played
badly, or could be someone sleeping – see **Nose**
whistle.)

YOU: (*sheepish*) Pssst. Ahoy there. Hello? It's me love. I
want to tell you something. Listen. I LOVE YOU,
and I've lost my keys. But I love you first and
foremost, lost keys very much in the second
position.
(*Pause. Silence.*)

YOU: Sweetheart. I know you're angry, but could you
please let me in? (*Then, remembering your Ace-in-*
the-Hole.) I've brought you a falafel. It's going cold.
(*Pause.*)

YOU: (*boldly*) Okay, now before you start woman – I
love you, and that clock's wrong.
(*Pause.*)

YOU: (*On your knees, weakly and shivering*) Please let me
in. I love you. Please. So very cold. Sleepy. I love
you. Falafel. Zzzzzzzzzz.

SHE: It's not locked, you idiot.

TIP Remember those mittens on elastic you had as an infant? Before you go out for the night, why not get your partner to attach your keys and your wallet to either end of a piece of wool, and thread it through the arms of your coat? It'll give muggers a fright too.

Love

What is love? It's that feeling you get in your guts when you see a girl across a crowded room and think, 'Wow. One day I'm going to make you the unhappiest woman alive.'

TIP 1 The key to lasting love is not how beautiful, successful or sexy your partner is, but whether they make you laugh. So do look out for opportunities to see your loved one falling off buses, tripping down the stairs of busy restaurants or getting amusingly caught on barbed wire fences.

TIP 2 Try not to mistake love for lust, which is worth four points less in Scrabble.

M

Making decisions together

One of the more splendid aspects of living with another cognisant human being, and involving them in day-to-day decision-making, is that it provides you with someone to blame when those decisions turn out rotten and expensive.

In the early stages of the relationship, shared decision-making is a fun activity. Later it may become less so, when you find yourself being asked to decide between the Cobalt blue in soft sheen and the Azure blue in matt for the cupboard under the stairs no one goes in.

Making decisions alone
Don't even think about it.

Things your partner might think you should not be left alone to choose:

- The brand/quality of toilet paper. 'Mr Rough's Recycled Economy tissue?'
- The evening's video entertainment.
- The babysitter. 'You met him in which pub?'
- The children's names. 'Pele?'
- Greeting cards. 'Padded pink satin?'
- When it's time to change the bed sheets. 'It's like sleeping on a crisp packet.'
- The ambient temperature of the home. 'I can see my breath!'
- The clothes you wear to a party. 'Take the tank top off.'

Things you might believe your partner should not decide alone:

- Any type of stereo equipment. 'Who the hell are Tingo?'
- The evening's video entertainment.
- Anything with an engine. 'It smokes a bit but you really liked the colour?'
- The dog's name. 'Fluffles?'
- Who to ask for directions. 'Those skinheads look local.'
- The ambient temperature of the home. 'I'm melting.'
- When it's time to leave a party. 'Please love, they're dressing their kids for school.'

Making up (*see also* Furniture, etc.)

For some people, this is by far the best part of the relationship, when all the hateful, bruising words are put aside, the tears and snot are wiped away, and she smartens herself up as well.

Masturbation

We both know it's a fallacy that males stop masturbating after seventeen. Most usually stop after one. However, if you are going to engage in this activity, be careful. Your partner is nobody's fool. If she suspects that you are using the shed for something a little racier than model Spitfire making, then one day she might ask you (by way of a test) to perform conjugal relations, just to make sure you're not 'empty'.

Do women masturbate? *See* Flatulence

Meanness

A couple of generations ago you would have been expected to hand over your wage packet to the woman of the household at the end of each week. (We must have caught them napping when we cancelled *that* cosy little set-up.) However, if you think you can maintain a relationship and keep all your earnings for yourself then you're in for a bit of a shock (*see* Bills, Joint accounts, Change, Gifts, Xmas, Washing).

Are you a tight git? Try this simple test.

- When friends in the pub ask you if you would like a drink you reply, 'No thanks, can I just have the money?' (20 points)

- You can get cigarettes out of your pocket one at a time at parties. Already lit. (10 points)

- You and your partner are learning Greek and Hebrew because you've got cable TV and they're the free channels. (20 points)

- You demand to know why lights are being used in the house when it's a full moon outside. (10 points)

- When someone shouts out, 'Thanks for the tip you tight twat,' you automatically turn round. (25 points)

- Your partner/family/friends refer to you as 'that tight-arsed bastard in the lounge'. (50 points)

TIP Remember – You're not mean, you're careful.

Mind games

Before engaging your partner in clever mind games, remember: Winston Churchill once said, 'A woman is an enigma, surrounded by a conundrum, wrapped in a duvet.' Well, almost. Or, 'A woman is like a Rubik's cube – you'll get one side right only to discover everything else will now be wrong.' (That's one of mine.)

Morning breath

If you haven't had the pleasure of waking up next to one another before (which I doubt, but it's not for me to pry) and have not yet experienced the full stinky aroma (which can be like opening a hot oven containing the bodies of several long dead rodents) of a breathily delivered, 'Morning darling. Great party. Do you fancy a shag?' followed by a bone-crunching squeeze and a putrid, furry tongue swept around your own tobacco and liquor-pickled gums, then your love is in for one of its sternest tests. (*See also* **True tests of love.**)

TIP If your partner's breath is particularly 'gamey' in the morning, when they get close, try doing that breathing just through your mouth trick that you learned when passing through smelly parts of the countryside or when visiting your granny's house.

DID YOU KNOW? It is a medical fact that you can tell the sex of someone to a 95 per cent accuracy just by the smell of their breath. Although you should really have checked before you let them get that close.

N

Nagging

Instead of nagging (which, in the attractiveness stakes, is up there with meanness and that corrugated line around your ankle left by too-tight socks), why not simply photocopy the following pages and hand them to your loved one each morning? That way it's dealt with, and you can enjoy the rest of your day together:

Stop doing that, what time do you call this, put your bicycle helmet on, slow down, wear a seatbelt, finish your tea, smarten yourself up, you never invite me, where's that going, don't force it, take it upstairs, bring it down, give me a hand, comb your hair, wipe your feet, put it down, pick it up, don't lose it, leave it there, go inside, get out, hurry up, don't forget, what have I told you, why didn't you tell me, look it up, write it down, ask them, is that it, blow your nose, wash your hands, cut your nails, were you born in a barn, give it to me, take it away, we never go out, don't eat before dinner, you never buy me flowers, don't speak to me like that, you're wasting your time, I told you this would happen, you never said it was going to be like this, let's turn back, keep going, why can't you stick at anything, I'm cold, I'm hot, what are you doing now, what do you think you're doing, don't even think about it, your trouble is you don't think, what were you thinking of, use the instruction book, you'll break it, you'll hurt it, you'll catch your death, do you have to make so much noise, don't sneak about, turn it up, turn it down, are you deaf, are you blind, are you stupid, are you still here, you're never here, take it off, put it on, you'll have someone's eye out with that, don't come crying to me, don't come, I might as well do it myself, do it later, do it now, do it properly, let's do it again, watch my ornaments, watch my hair, mind the paintwork, you'll hurt yourself, you'll kill us all, was that you, why is it always me, what have you been doing, I told you not to, don't eat with your mouth open, don't talk when you're eating, don't eat it in here, don't eat it all, you'd better eat it all, why do you have to be different, stop showing off, stop showing me up, don't do it like that, turn the light off, shut the door, close the fridge, don't waste the battery, get off there, don't make a mess, who's made this mess, stop messing me about, hand it over, cut it out, let me try, get off me, why can't you, why don't you, why haven't you, what do I know, don't tell me, tell me, don't pick it, don't scratch it, don't pull it, say pardon, open a window, use a hankie, don't wipe it there, get your feet off, get out from under my feet, get down from there, get off your arse, get over it, why do I have to tell you twice, I'm not telling you again, not that one, put it back, turn it over, come to bed, get to bed, get out of that bed, *stop nagging me.*

78 Nagging

Neighbours

You should think about staying on the right side of these people. They can be very useful if you need your hedge cutting, your parcels taken in when you are not at home, or if you want them to keep quiet about your sexual performance (*see* **Noises (sexual)**).

Nightmares

Depending on your luck another name for your friends or her parents.

Noises (sexual)

One of the major luxuries of having your own home is that now you can both really let yourselves go on the love-making noise front. No longer will you have to live in fear of being disturbed in the communal lounge by angry flat-mates, desperate for sleep, who burst in and shout, 'Keep the bloody noise down and do you mind, some of us eat off that coffee table.'

More! More!
It's fair to say that your partner's 'seagull' noises are more arousing than your own 'warthog breaking cover' efforts (although I've heard neither, honest). However, some wanton cries can venture into the hurtful . . .

SHE: (*writhing*) Yes, that's the spot. Keep going. Oh wow. That's it. More, more.

YOU: Okay baby (*puff*). You like that, do you? (*wheeze*) Do you baby?

SHE: Yes, yes. More, more.

YOU: Okay, here it is. Don't pull my hair quite so hard please, love.

SHE: Yes, yes.

YOU: Okay. Just loosen your grip a bit will you. OK here it is, if you can take it?

SHE: Oh yes, more, more.

YOU: Okay! (*pant*)

SHE: More, more. (*louder and louder*) More, more.

YOU: (*disturbed*) Okay.

SHE: (*to a crescendo*) More, more, more, more.

YOU: (*irritated*) 'Hey, can you stop with the more, more's? There is no bloody more. If there was any more I would gladly give it to you.

SHE: (*calming down*) Damn. I nearly came then.

YOU: Well I'm sorry love. It was the 'more, more' thing. You were putting me off.

SHE: Sorry. I was enjoying myself.

YOU: I know, but couldn't you shout 'less, less'? The neighbours are listening. I have to face these people.

SHE: I guess so.

YOU: Thanks.

SHE: Anything else?

YOU: I'd quite like a car.

Non-verbal communication – what does it all mean?

Hers:

- Sigh – You haven't noticed something new about her appearance.
- Tut – You *have* noticed something but that wasn't it.
- Folded arms – You've said something in the past fortnight, she's gone away and thought about it, and has decided she doesn't like it. Now she is waiting for you to a) guess what it is, and b) apologise for it. To spice things up, she has also decided that she is not going to give you any clues as to what it may be.
- Folded arms when vacuuming – Neat trick.
- Smirk – She's enjoying watching you try to guess why she's annoyed with you, thus giving her some fresh reasons to be annoyed. It's the perfect lose, lose situation.
- Raised eyebrow – She's having trouble believing that what she caught you doing in the shed was a very important prostate self-examination and that you were holding your penis in your other hand for balance.
- Raised eyebrow with smirk – She thinks you could do with some extra lessons in foreplay technique at night school.
- Punch to the arm – She's spotted you ogling women from behind your sunglasses.
- Slap around face – She hasn't found coming back from the bathroom to find all the remaining pizza slices stuffed inside your mouth as funny as you thought.

- Weeping – She's happy, sad, who knows?

His:
- Sigh – He's not happy that you've kept him to a promise he made when he was drunk.
- Tut – He's remembered something he could be doing now if you weren't being quite so unreasonable.
- Arms folded – There's an attractive woman in the vicinity and he doesn't want her to see his belly.
- Smirk – He's just let off and can hear someone else getting the blame for it.
- Raised eyebrow – He's having trouble believing you've somehow lost the receipt for those new shoes.
- Raised eyebrow with a smirk – He's remembered what you promised to do when you were drunk.
- Punch in the arm – He's just got the phone bill.
- Slap around the face – He's concerned your hysteria about the phone bill is getting out of hand.
- Weeping – He'd quite like a car.

Nose whistle

Oddly annoying two-tone sound emitted from one nostril during sleep when the other one is blocked by snot/your finger/the cat's bum. (*See also* **Snoring**.)

Notes

In the early stages of a relationship, expect to find the house festooned with cute little notes and smiley faces containing such information as, 'Gone to the toilet, love you', 'I'm in the bath, wake me if I've gone under' and 'Sally (with the big fucking boobs!) called. PS Where are these free kittens?'

Later you'll be lucky if you get an envelope scrap nailed to the bathroom door with 'Piss off, I'm having my period', scrawled on it.

O

Opening jars

This, and the occasional ejection of a daddy long legs from the bedroom, for some reason makes you irresistible to the opposite sex, or at least raises your stock above the vibrator. (*See also* **Trade offs**.)

Opinions (*see also* Zilch)

It's best to appreciate early on that in certain areas, such as nutrition, a fair price for a pair of shoes, and the volume at which the sound track to *Moulin Rouge* should be played in the car, your views aren't worth a carrot.

TIP Try sneaking your own opinions into the conversation as things you read this month in *Cosmopolitan*.

Oral sex (*see also* Grovelling)

Of course the big question here is, how long to do it for? For women the answer is pretty easy, but for men, taking as long over it as you would a postage stamp is frowned upon. Therefore, to avoid friction and to strengthen your relationship immeasurably, I suggest getting your snorkel out, putting *Tubular Bells* on the hifi, and cancelling the milk.

'Our stuff' – say goodbye to 'your' belongings

When you move in with someone, you will find some of your most treasured items magically become '*our* stuff'. This can be cute and endearing to start, and can help with early bonding, but then, one day, you'll see her decorating in your best jumper WITHOUT ASKING and you'll wish her ill.

YOU: Hey, is that one of my jumpers?

SHE: I think so.

YOU: What do you mean, 'you think so'? Would you have bought a sweater with 'I've got a big knob' on the front?

SHE: Probably not. I don't know whose it is. I just found it in the bedroom. Do you think it suits me? (*Cue: jumper pulled down to knees and placating cute twirl.*)

YOU: (*alarmed*) You're stretching it. Stop it. You know it's not old, I had it on yesterday and you said you really liked it.

SHE: Did I?

YOU: Yes. Look, you've got something on the arm. Is it paint?

SHE: (*giggle*) Maybe. Oh no, I wiped my nose on it. (*More giggles.*) So this isn't one of your old ones?

YOU: You know it's not.

SHE: (*sheepish*) I'll put it back then.

YOU: Yes please.

(*She removes jumper.*)

YOU: Hey, are they my underpants?

SHE: Oops.

YOU: Oh for God's sake.

P

Parents

Love them, hate them, you can't beat their splendid free curtain-making skills and superb unpaid furniture-removal abilities. Also a very good reminder of what you and your partner will turn out like (if you're not *very* careful).

Are you turning into your parents?

- You're heard saying, 'Let's take a packed lunch, I'm not paying café prices.'
- You can't go past a field of lambs without saying, 'They'd be lovely with some mint sauce,' or some other *hilarious* quip.
- You keep a screwed-up hankie handy, ready to gob on in case you need to clean the face of a small child.
- You force several pounds of sugared almonds on to unfortunate houseguests.
- You start buying salad cream because you reckon it's the same as mayonnaise.

Parties (*see also* Alcohol, Arguments, etc.)

> **TIP** When it's your turn to drive home from a party and you sincerely want to get drunk, try drinking four glasses of wine really quickly upon arrival and then saying, 'Oh damn. I forgot it was my turn.'

Party invitations

You will be failing in your duty as a man if you don't 'helpfully' pick these up from the mantelpiece a few moments before leaving the house, and then miraculously lose them forever.

Passing on messages

The rule here is: Don't answer the phone. Ever. If you do, you will get involved in message taking, which is a discipline you will *never* manage to perform to her satisfaction. You will inevitably take down not enough information, or the wrong information, or the right information but in bad writing; you'll either give away too much to the other person or not pass on something you should have. So don't even try.

The reason message taking is so fraught with danger is because your partner lives in a completely different world from you. Whereas your dealings with friends and colleagues are simple and direct (some might say, bordering on the curt), her relationships are cloaked in politics, mystery, doublespeak and subterfuge. When *you* pick up the phone, you enter this world and frankly, you can't win:

(*Sound of clock striking four p.m.*)

SHE: (*emerging in pyjama top, hair like Don King*)
Morning, any messages?

YOU: Someone called around lunchtime – a bloke called Dave Hartington?

SHE: Who's that?

YOU: I've no idea. Said it was something about work. He wants you to send him a CV.

SHE: (*worried*) Did he ask to speak to me?

YOU: Yes.

SHE: What did you tell him?

YOU: I said you were in bed.

SHE: You said I was in bed? You idiot. What did you tell him that for?

YOU: Because you were in bed.

SHE: I know I was, but you didn't have to tell him that. He's the guy I've got an interview with next week. What's he going to think of me now? Still in bed at lunchtime. Shit! He's going to think I'm some lazy lump who lies in bed all day.

YOU: Well I've done you a favour, now you won't have to lie on your CV.

(*Sound of phone ringing.*)

YOU: Hello?

FRIEND: Is she there?

YOU: Hello yourself. She's in the bath.

FRIEND: Is she going to be long?

YOU: She got in a couple of hours ago so she'll probably just be another hour.

FRIEND: Okay. Will you tell her – it's Christine here by the way – will you tell her there's been a change of plan? We're going to The Snooty Fox for a drink first . . . do you want to write this down?

YOU: No.

FRIEND: Will you remember it all?

YOU: (*lying*) Yes.

FRIEND: OK, then we're going to pick up Sue at about half eight, drop the presents off, meet Angie at the Fart and Foreskin . . . It's called the Fleece and Firkin, but that's our joke. (*Pause.*) Hello?

YOU: Yes.

SHE: So then we'll all go on from there. But – and I know she's going to go mad about this – tell her, Elaine Fernley's coming as well. Sue, the big mouth, invited her. It's a massive cock-up, but it's nothing to do with me. So tell her, if she still wants to come, I'll meet her at Snooty's at eight. But if she doesn't because of the problem with Elaine, who isn't even supposed to be talking to Sue so I don't know how *that* happened, I'll understand. Have you got all that?

YOU: Yes. Bye.

FRIEND: Bye.

(*Pause.*)

SHE: (*shouting from upstairs*) Who was that on the phone?

YOU: (*shouting back*) Some nutcase called Christine.

SHE: What did she say?

YOU: She said she'll see you there.

Passing on your 'love'

SHE: I'm popping in to see Mark and Julie on the way home; shall I give them your love?

YOU: No thank you.

SHE: Why not?

YOU: I don't think I'm ready for that kind of commitment.

Personal space

For you, the shed, the attic, or any other cold, damp, spider-infested place. For her, the warm, perfumed womb that is the bathroom.

Pets (*see also* Cats)

Before allowing dogs to sleep in your bedroom remember, they don't break wind, they smash it. (*See also* **Revenge**.)

PMT (Pre-Menstrual Tension)

A time of heightened emotions, just before the start of your girlfriend's period, when you may notice her sobbing uncontrollably over a dead snail found on the footpath, or threatening to leave you for making eye contact with an elderly lollypop lady.

Pyjamas

One pair is enough for two. It is tradition that she gets the top and you get the bottom. You may also get to learn what that top pocket is for.

Q

Questions

- Have you ever . . .?
- Would you ever . . .?
- When did you first . . .?
- If she and I were in different rooms . . .?
- Do you think I'd suit . . .?

REMEMBER: No matter how casually or politely asked, never, *ever* answer questions that start with these words honestly. *Ever.*

Twenty Questions – A fun game to play in the car on the way home from a party:

YOU: What's wrong?
SHE: Nothing.
YOU: What's wrong?
SHE: Nothing.
YOU: What's wrong?
SHE: Nothing.
YOU: There is. There's something wrong, what is it?

SHE: There's nothing wrong.

YOU: Yes there is, what is it?

SHE: Nothing.

YOU: What's wrong?

SHE: Nothing.

YOU: Tell me. What is it?

SHE: Look, I shouldn't have to tell you, you should know.

YOU: So there is something wrong?

SHE: There's nothing wrong.

YOU: What's wrong?

SHE: Nothing.

YOU: What's wrong?

SHE: Nothing.

YOU: What's wrong?

SHE: Nothing.

YOU: How long is this going to go on for?

SHE: There's nothing wrong.

YOU: What's wrong?

SHE: Nothing.

YOU: Then why have you got a face like you've just chewed a paracetemol?

SHE: I haven't.

YOU: You have. What's wrong?

SHE: Nothing.

YOU: What's wrong?

SHE: Nothing.

YOU: What's wrong?

SHE: Nothing.

YOU: What's wrong?

SHE: Nothing.

YOU: What's wrong?

SHE: It doesn't matter.

YOU: What?

(Pause)

SHE: Nothing.

YOU: I give up.

Quickies – 'As opposed to what?'

We all like sex. It's a great way to clear a blocked nose. However, unlike loafers such as Sting, we don't need to do it for nine hours at a stretch. Surely sex should be a thrilling fairground ride, not a coach trip to Carlisle (or some other comedy place nine hours from where you live).

Of course, now that you are living together, as opposed to just visiting for knee-dislocating, late-night sofa-sex, there's no excuse for not taking your time, possibly even engaging in *minutes* of sexual activity.

If, however, your partner is one of those scary people who demands eight hours of foreplay (think of your knees), followed by nine hours of tantric silliness, then you may want to think of secret ways to limit the time given over to sex. For example, try initiating sex a few moments before the start of her favourite TV programme:

YOU: Oh baby, this is wonderful.

SHE: Is it in?

YOU: You bet. (*Pant*) Wow, this is good for me.

SHE: I can't feel anything. I think I need to align my meridians.

YOU: Whatever it takes sweetheart.

SHE: Can you stop bobbing for a moment? I'm trying to concentrate on my Chakras.

YOU: Sorry darling. I'm just on fire tonight.

SHE: If you don't slow it down a bit, you'll come before the paperboy.

YOU: I'll do my best, love, it's just that I feel so lucky that we're lovers and not just (*right in her ear*) *Friends*.

SHE: *Friends*? Oh bugger. What time is it?

YOU: Nine o'clock, maybe?

SHE: Right, hurry up. I need to put the telly on.

YOU: Okay. But don't call *me* the unromantic one again.

R

Reassurance

The reason for all those odd mind games, which leave you totally confused and lost for words when she says to you, half way through a post-coital cuddle, that she doesn't think you fancy her anymore.

R.E.S.P.E.C.T.

Very important aspect of any relationship, earned when both parties show love, understanding and a deep commitment to one another. Failing that can also be bought with hard cash.

Revenge

Ways for you and your partner to get back at each other:

- Turn on the hot tap downstairs while the other is in the shower, to give them an icy reminder of your disgruntlement.
- Eat a large pickled egg before bed.
- Leave a friend's 'positive' pregnancy test result in the bathroom. (Men – don't try this one.)
- Write 'Kick me' in UV marker on the back of any garments they intend to wear to a nightclub.
- Feed the dog a large bowl of wet grass just before your partner takes it on a long car journey.

Romance (*see also* Candles, G-strings)

It is very easy to get bogged down in the routine of life, and forget that all relationships must be worked at to keep them from becoming stale and predictable (*see* **Boredom**). So on Valentine's Day, why not give her a surprise she'll never forget? Go out with your mates instead.

Romantic weekend breaks – 'Please love, leave them a teabag!'

YOU: Do you fancy a romantic weekend break away?
SHE: Sure, I could do with some new towels.

You can't beat a romantic stay in a luxury hotel to indulge two of her favourite passions – cuddling and kleptomania.

For some reason, normally decent, honest women become raging Artful Dodgers when tempted by unscrewed-down hotel fixtures and fittings. Shampoo sachets, soaps, shower caps, towels, tissues, sewing kits, shoe-shine kits, toilet rolls – both the one in use and the 'spare', light bulbs, flannels, feminine hygiene bags and pot pourri displays will all be 'hoovered' up at the end of any stay.

Is your partner's hotel kleptomania getting out of hand?

- She's spotted dragging the hotel bed down the corridor whilst saying, 'It's not theft, this is complimentary.'
- Guests to your home notice each room has its own Corby trouser press.
- Your neighbours complain that the wind flapping through the flags of the thirteen member states of the EEC lined up in your garden is keeping them awake.
- All your family photos are in Employee of the Month frames.

S

Sanitary products

'Oh, and can you get me some tampons?'

A lot of men understandably get freaked out when this request comes their way. And the annoying thing is you can't hit back with a request of your own. Nothing you could possibly ask her to buy would be anywhere near as embarrassing as the things she already purchases on a regular basis.

Tampon wrappers (plastic)
At first, you may think an unseen dwarf is living in your bathroom, smoking small cigars. Later, when you've tired of picking them off the floor or using them as target practice in the loo, you'll simply pray for a tidier girlfriend.

Tampon wrappers (paper)
Save these for when your hippie friends come round and run out of cigarette papers at three a.m.

Secrets

For a relationship to remain strong and healthy, it's very important that there are no secrets between you. Although do leave her the secret of where she goes to let off.

Selective blindness

Worrying mystery condition (usually brought on by the stress of getting ready for an important social function) that leaves her unable to see any of the clothes in her wardrobe. She is then left angry and confused that she has nothing to wear and so can't possibly go out. Ever. This condition is not eased by you helpfully informing her that you can see many perfectly good items of clothing in there.

Likewise you may be struck down with a similar disease, which affects your ability to see dirty underpants on the floor and when the kitchen bin needs emptying.

Selective hearing

Another stress-related mystery illness, brought on by, amongst other things, the worry caused by inviting annoying people to dinner without proper consultation:

(You are sitting at the table in the kitchen; your partner is putting away some recently purchased groceries. She has just told you who is coming to dinner tonight.)

YOU: *(shocked)* Who? Mark and Alison? When did this happen?

(Silence. She continues to put the food away.)

YOU: *(holding your forehead to lay on your acute distress at the news a bit more)* I don't believe it. You know I can't stand either of them. He's boring with dandruff on the inside of his glasses and she makes disgusting noises when she eats with her mouth open.

(Silence)

YOU: If they do come, I can't guarantee I won't vomit. In fact, do you know what I'm going to do? I'm going to vomit on her. How about that? I'll just say, 'Sorry about that, Alison, but the sound of you eating is so nauseating, that was an accident waiting to happen. To be honest, I'm surprised it doesn't happen to you more often.'

(Silence)

YOU: And then I'll say, 'No, Mark, I'm not interested in the chemical composition of human bile, why don't you shut up and clean your glasses, you tedious twat?' How about that for an evening?

(Silence)

YOU: *(noticing a suspicious packet amongst the groceries)* Is that sticky-toffee pudding? Oh no. What is she going to sound like when she eats that? We'll have next-door saying, 'Can you get your Rottweiller to eat that custard a little more quietly?'

(*Silence*)

YOU: Hello? Are you hearing all this?

(*Silence*)

YOU: (*to self*) Am I speaking? What's going on? I'm talking, I can hear sound, but it doesn't seem to be registering with those around me.

(*Silence*)

YOU: (*slumping into chair, defeated*) So what time are they coming round?

SHE: Eight o'clock.

YOU: Oh you heard that question. Right, I'll get the mop and bucket.

Sex – *see* Quickies, noises (sexual), Oral sex, etc.

Sharing (*see also* 'Our stuff')

One of the immediate, fun aspects of a relationship is sharing – late-night pizzas, bottles of wine, dirty secrets, more bottles of wine, more dirty secrets, hot, soapy showers, and then possibly body fluids.

It will take a little longer (or perhaps more alcohol) before you both appreciate sharing certain other things: the zapper, chewing gum, your savings.

NOTE It is not considered 'sharing' to only hand over the 'Business and Finance' section of the Sunday paper.

Shoes (hers)

As you gaze upon the rows of footwear in the hallway, you may be forgiven for thinking that you are now living with a fashion-conscious centipede. On certain occasions, of course, she can't see any of them. (*See* **Selective blindness**.)

Shopping

It is said that for some women, the experience of shopping is like sex. It could also be argued that shopping is like sex for men, too, which is why we can only manage it for about five minutes and then we get tired; whereas women can keep going for hours, getting purchase after multiple purchase.

TIP Avoid shopping for food when you're both hungry. With everything looking so tasty through low-blood-sugar eyes, you'll get home and have to make a well-balanced meal out of several packets of crisps, a few assorted pastry-based snacks and a couple of packets of Yo-Yos.

Showing her up

Apparently this is one of those things that she doesn't find amusing on any level.

Silence (*see also* Sulking)

Golden and terrifying.

What to do if you are getting the silent treatment: Rejoice! (That's a joke.)

Smells

What's that smell she leaves behind in the toilet? It's called disinfectant. Don't worry, it soon goes.

Smiling

Once a sign of happiness, now a sure-fire way to raise suspicion. Avoid being caught smiling when coming out of the bathroom, the shed, or the bank.

'Snuggles'

Dreamy higher state above 'Cuddles'.

Spiders (*see also* Trade-offs)

We both know it's a myth that men aren't afraid of spiders. Indeed, finding a big hairy one in the bath leads you secretly to wish that handguns were still legal in this country. However, like foot massages and changing electric plugs, removing spiders is one of those things someone in the house should learn to perform, if only for the incredible bargaining power it gives you:

YOU: There's a spider in the bath. Quick, phone the estate agents, we have to move.

SHE: A spider? How big?

YOU: Huge. You have to get rid of it.

SHE: Is it hairy?

YOU: Yes. Very.

SHE: And black and crawly?

YOU: Yes, yes. I thought I was going to die.

SHE: Sorry love. I'm busy watching TV.

YOU: Argh! Please. You have to.

SHE: I'm busy.

YOU: No. You can't be.

SHE: Well, if I did do it, not that I'm saying I would, but if I did, you know it would cost you.

YOU: Anything. Anything.

SHE: I'd quite like a car.

'Spoons'

A type of cutlery, and the musical instrument most favoured by drunken, toothless uncles at parties. Also the name for the sleeping method whereby she assumes the highly agreeable foetal position, while you attempt to curl in directly behind her. In doing so, you'll spend the night inhaling large quantities of her hair and trying to stop your head falling through the annoying gap in the pillows. Still, so long as she's comfortable, eh?

Sunday

The day God took off from creating the world to take Mrs God around IKEA.

T

Tank tops

If you want the relationship to last beyond your first summer, quietly bundle these up along with your white (with a hint of pink) cut-off jeans, your 'So Many Women – So Little Time' T-shirts and your cowboy boots, and set them on fire.

The telephone (*see also* Arguments, Passing on messages, Meanness)

Unfortunately, everything that has ever been said about women and telephones is true. So welcome to the world of: 'It's not for you', 'Put it down, I'm using it', 'As a matter of fact, Mum called *me*', and 'Hurry up and get off it, I'm expecting a call'.

If you're in any doubt that your partner has a love affair with the telephone, witness her reaction to the bill arriving and how her emotions mirror the six classic stages of grieving response to a broken romance:

SHOCK:	How can it be so much?
DENIAL:	I never made all those calls.
ANGER:	How dare they charge so much for a stupid phone call?
BARGAINING:	If you let me off this time, I promise I'll start putting money in that little jar in the future.
BLAME:	It's all their fault. Those bitches never phone me.
REMORSE:	I'm so sorry. I think I have an illness. Actually it's probably best that you rip the damn thing out because I've decided I'm not going to use it ever again. In fact I'm going to call everyone I know straight away to tell them I'm no longer contactable by phone.

Things . . .

Things you'll never hear a woman say
- My, what an attractive scrotum.
- I've packed too many clothes for holiday.
- A hairy back – lovely.
- That's enough foreplay.
- I couldn't eat another chocolate.
- …….………………….………..[*Reader to add own here*]
- …….………………….………..[*Reader to add own here*]

Things you'll never hear a man say
- Oral sex . . .? No thank you.
- Could you pass me the clothes pegs, please?
- I'm sorry darling, could you tell me that again, but in a bit more detail?
- …….………………….………..[*Reader to add own here*]
- …….………………….………..[*Reader to add own here*]

Tights (aka pantyhose)

Along with mind reading, one of the many life skills you will need to acquire is the ability to unbraid your washing from your partner's tights, which, after a wash and spin, wrap around your clothes like a terrified octopus.

Toenails

It might have been okay to have toenails that can pick up small rodents from the undergrowth when you were single, and all you had to worry about was laddering your nylon sheets, but they are frowned upon when you are sharing a bed with someone on a regular basis. It can be taxing, catching all the brittle bits that ping over the kitchen, but it is much better than slicing open your girl-friend's calf during one of those funny little involuntary muscular twitches you get just as you're nodding off.

Toilet paper

After you've found yourself trying to wipe your bum using the meticulously unravelled inner cardboard tube a few times, it might dawn on you that the household usage of toilet paper has rocketed somewhat since your partner arrived on the domestic scene. This is in part due to the multitudinous uses she has for this material:

- Handkerchief
- Makeup removing rag
- Sterile toilet seat barrier or padded bum-protector
- Excess lipstick remover
- Earplugs
- Emergency breast implants

Questions worth asking your partner after your thirty-seventh trip to the corner shop for loo roll replenishment:

- Do you know if there are any giant hamsters living in or around our property?
- Have you seen any Labrador puppies legging it away from our home?
- Do you go to a lot of football matches?

Toiletries

The name for those expensive creams, potions, exfoliates and unguents that you can't help notice give her a complexion no better than the one you get with washing-up liquid.

Trade-offs

The best way to allocate those jobs around the home that you both hate is to apply a simple points system. That way, there are no arguments over who does what:

Putting rubbish out (sunshine)	3 pts
Putting rubbish out (rain)	6 pts
Answering phone (family members)	3 pts
Answering phone (unpopular friends)	8 pts
Saying you're not in/in bath/moved away	10 pts
Unblocking bath/sink	7 pts
Unblocking bath/sink (if hair involved)	12 pts

Unblocking loo	price on application
Emptying vacuum cleaner	8 pts
Cleaning bottom of toothbrush holder	6 pts
Driving to a party	5 pts
Driving from a party	20 pts
Driving from a party if 'out of turn'	40pts
Making tea	3 pts
Bringing tea in bed	6 pts
Answering door to carol singers	4 pts
Answering door to 'trick or treaters'	6 pts
Answering door to salespeople/religious nuts	10 pts
Taking something back on behalf of the other person	5 pts
Taking something back on behalf of the other person (no receipt)	10 pts
Phoning in sick	5 pts
Phoning in sick (bogus)	10 pts
Opening jars (depending on stiffness)	2–5 pts
Cleaning up vomit (human)	12 pts
Cleaning up vomit (animal)	15 pts
Cleaning up vomit (unknown)	20 pts
Eviction of insects and small animals:	
Spider (dead)	1 pt
Spider (alive)	6 pts
Moth (stationary)	1 pt
Moth (flying)	3 pts
Daddy longlegs	2 pts
Wasp	6 pts
Bee	4 pts

Beetle (attractive, e.g. ladybird)	1 pt
Beetle (ugly, e.g. woodlouse)	2 pts
Mouse	20 pts
Rat	30 pts
Wild bird	40 pts
Investigation of intruder (imagined)	8 pts
Investigation of intruder (real)	50 pts
	+ hospital bills

True tests of love (*see also* Morning breath)

It is inevitable that, over time, you and your partner will reveal things to each other – possibly by accident – that will test the strength of that love bond between you. These include:

- Holiday diarrhoea.
- Fainting in a crowded pub.
- Their relaxed Sunday attire.
- Expulsion of chewing-gum/lager from their mouth/ nose during a laughing fit.
- Saying the word 'yummy'.
- Seeing school photos of them without teeth.
- Emerging from a snorkelling trip with the mask imprint on their face and three inches of snot hanging from their nose.
- Watching them finish a half-marathon, bandy-legged and wrapped in a space blanket.

Underpants

Every man knows that a good canvas pair could, if necessary, be pressed into service for about a month – front one week, then turn them round for another week, then inside out, and finally round again. Sadly this method doesn't work for jeans or business suits.

TIP When you're tucking your shirt into your underpants, it's time to shuffle off your mortal coil.

Uses for men's old underpants:
- Cleaning rags
- Amusing exhibit to break the ice at home dinner parties.
- Warning to children about the dangers of combining alcohol with Asian food.
- Hoist for evacuating large groups of people from burning buildings.
- Hat for a unicorn.

TIP When decommissioning your underpants, ask your partner to cut them into small pieces, to remove any temptation to use them again as emergency spares even though they do smell of Pledge.

Under the stairs

That place where you store the vacuum cleaner and which everyone knows should be painted in matt Azure blue.

Utensils

TIP When you find yourself eating your cornflakes with a ladle, it's time to do the washing up.

U-turns

Something she never really learns to enjoy you doing on a busy dual carriageway.

V

Vaginal flatulence

Quite simply, one of God's 'amusing' little jokes. Caused by trapped air releasing noisily after (and sometimes, disconcertingly, *during*) sex. If you haven't encountered this phenomenon, just imagine the sound of a Wellington boot being pulled slowly from the mud. Usually followed immediately by an embarrassed, 'Oops'.

If you don't laugh, cry or emigrate afterwards, your relationship will be all the stronger for living through it.

Things to say to lighten the moment:
- I think next-door's Harley Davidson needs a service.
- You must teach me how to do that; it's the rugby club reunion dinner next week.
- Was that your hot water bottle or mine?
- Oh no! I think we're under attack from killer blamanches.

Videos (rental) (*see also* Arguments, Making decisions, Compromise, etc.)

Videos are the mainstay of most modern relationships. You can expect to increase your video watching by 2000% or 3000% when you start living together. Well, at least they're not fattening.

What to watch?

A well-known area of conflict between couples is deciding what video to watch on that romantic night in. It is unlikely that you share the same tastes, so it is a good idea to rent two videos at a time, say, one action, one romance (although you might not always choose a romance). This should keep you both happy. However, if you wish to watch both films that evening, beware this sneaky female tactic:

YOU: Okay, which one do you want to watch?

SHE: Let's watch my one first.

YOU: Okay, *The Kissers* it is. Are you sure this is good?

SHE: It got five stars in [*insert name of some film magazine you've never heard of here*].

YOU: Can't argue with that.
(*You both watch the film. End credits roll.*)

YOU: What a load of bollocks!

SHE: Brilliant.

YOU: Which film were you watching?

SHE: You're such a cynic.

YOU: Are you crying?

SHE: (*looking away*) Don't be silly. (*Sniffle.*) I've got popcorn in my eye.

YOU: Okay. Now for our second feature presentation – Mr Jackie Chan in—

SHE: I'm off to bed now.

YOU: Aah-hh! Please stay up, love. I get lonely on my own.

SHE: I hate Jackie Chan.

YOU: But this one's a romance, I think.

SHE: What's it called?

YOU: Erm, *I'm Going To Punch Your Lights Out – In Paris.*

W

Washing (clothes)

You must do all your own clothes washing. It may be tempting to take advantage of your partner's innate knowledge of washing symbols (You: Apparently I'm supposed to keep this garment away from triangles), but it is a brave man who leaves anything in his pockets on washday. Anything found is considered a 'cleaner's perk' and any coins, notes, jewellery, eternity rings, or bad pictures of her that you keep in your wallet, will not be returned.

Washing (-up)

Buy a dishwasher, or do the job so badly that you're not asked to do it again. Among the classics is to 'accidentally' break a couple of the best wineglasses each time you dip your hands into the sink. Eventually your dinner guests will be toasting each other out of assorted teacups and that dusty tankard you won at darts (*see* **Knick-knacks**). Then whenever there's washing-up to be done you'll be told to go and sit down quietly out of the way.

Waxing

Method used to achieve weird and wonderful shapes to the female pubic region, whereby hot wax is poured over the area then the hairs are ripped from the body using something akin to gaffer tape (feel free to sit down at this point). Interestingly, the skin left behind at the top of the inner thigh can sometimes resemble a line of perfect Braille – hence Bikini *Line* (although it would be unwise to mention this).

> **TIP** For obvious, physical reasons, your own attempts at pubic topiary will be limited, but it is feasible to surprise her on her birthday with your pubic hair shaped into a couple of eyebrows.
>
> YOU: **What do you think of my Groucho?**
> SHE: **Didn't he have a bigger cigar than that?**

Wet towels

We both know that the best place for these is on the bed, preferably an un-made bed so that the dampness can spread into the sheets and mattress. However, you may find your partner doesn't care for this behaviour. Therefore, save it for when she leaves you '**home alone**'.

X

Xmas

If one occasion highlights how much your life has been transformed by living with your partner, then it has to be Christmas. No longer for you the single person misery of Christmas day turkey burger and chips, a single card on the mantelpiece – from you, one solitary piece of limp tinsel hanging from the bare light bulb from the ceiling, pulling Christmas crackers wedged into the door, the despair when the door wins, and the loneliness of tugging yourself off to Billy Smart's Circus before finally falling asleep face down in a pool of your own vomit, while the chip-pan catches fire in the kitchen. (What a shame those days had to end.)

> **TIP 1** Avoid purchasing your Christmas presents at the last minute. Gifts from the 24-hour garage are rarely appreciated as much as those from Harrods or even Woolworth's, and unwrapping a litre of two-stroke oil or a Cornish pastie on Christmas morning will test the blindest love.

TIP 2 If you have been forced to attend a tedious family 'bash', a good way to brighten it up is to tell your own rude mottos and pass them off as ones from the Christmas crackers. For example, pull the cracker, then pick up the piece of paper with the 'joke' on it and say, 'Okay, let me read you the motto . . . here we are: 'What's the worst thing about having a lung transplant?' Wait for people to guess. Then answer, 'Having to bring up someone else's phlegm.' Repeat until told to leave the house.

X-rated videos

If, when you gather all your single man pornographic material into one place, the words 'Emporium' or 'Porn Baron' spring to mind, as a mark of respect to your partner you might want to consider thinning your collection.

Excuses that ought to work but don't:
- Look, it's the most natural act in the world.
- The donkey doesn't seem to mind.
- I swear it was bought in error. I didn't realise it was called *Chitty Chitty Gang Bang*.

Yes

The correct answer to the following questions:

- If I were in a wheelchair would you look after me?
- Do you love me more than you love the cat?
- You know I only ran away because I'm a pacifist, don't you?
- Am I the best you've had?
- Would you love me if I had no money?
- Are we having Rice Krispie chocolate crackles for tea tonight?

Your buttocks

It may come to your notice that since moving in with your partner, your backside has acquired many new and varied uses. These include:

- Foot warmer
- Magazine rack for Sunday newspapers
- Hilarious Sunday morning raspberry noise-maker
- Stress reliever
- Car door closer (when carrying several bags of shopping)
- Any bad smells whipping boy

Z

Zapper (aka remote control)

I know there ought to be a law somewhere that says that all remote controls belong solely to you. I know it's frustrating that your partner takes so long to flick through the channels, what with her constant stopping each time she comes across someone crying, kissing passionately, or stroking an injured animal.

> **TIP** If you need to visit the loo and have to leave the remote control unattended for any length of time, take the batteries out.

Zilch

If you're a man, this is the sum total you will receive of the following:

- Respect: for your tears when *you* have nothing to wear to a posh party.
- Appreciation: for *your* monthly stomach pain.
- Sympathy: if *you're* chatted up in the pub.
- Pity: if you lose *your* eyelashes at a barbeque.
- Flowers: if *she* comes home late.
- ....[*Reader to add own here*]

But then, who said life was fair?

Zips

You may wonder just how she managed to do her dresses up when you weren't around. Maybe the guy who opened all the pickle jars and got stuff down from the high shelves did it.

Zzzzz (aka snoring – *see also* Nose whistle)

If you are living with a snorer it is important that you learn to 'tune out', otherwise you may find it puts you off your orgasm.

Author's note

Although every endeavour has been made to ensure that the entries contained herein are the funniest ones possible the author could think of for the money, it is accepted there are probably many more that he hasn't noticed or simply couldn't be arsed to write down. For this reason, a website dedicated to readers' own suggestions for A–Z entries has been set up. Feel free to visit it and add your own personal offerings at:

www.A-ZofLivingTogether.com

Acknowledgements

My deepest thanks go to Miles Ross for helping with the original idea and giving me valuable feedback, to Addison Cresswell for telling me to write it, to Joe and all at Off the Kerb for their kind support, to Antonia Hodgson at Time Warner for her C.B.F. (Could Be Funnier) notes, and to Adrian Bohm for lending me a place to plug in my laptop. And of course to all the women I've ever dated (although the number isn't as impressive as that makes it sound) – none of whom has provided inspiration for any of the entries in this book . . .